OSCOLA Ireland
Second Edition

legalcitation.ie

This citation guide is based on OSCOLA which was devised by the Faculty of Law at Oxford University and we are grateful for their permission to adapt it for the purposes of developing a standard citation style for Ireland.

Copyright © 2016 by Larry Donnelly, Elaine Fahey, Rónán Kennedy, and Jennifer Schweppe

This work is distributed under an Attribution-NonCommercial-ShareAlike 3.0 Ireland (CC BY-NC-SA 3.0 IE) licence. For more information, see https://creativecommons.org/licenses/by-nc-sa/3.0/ie/

Printed by Lulu.com

ISBN 978-1-365-07547-6

Published by LegalCitation.ie

Contents

Introduction 1
1 General notes 3
   1.1   Citations and footnotes...3
       1.1.1   Citing cases 3
       1.1.2   Citing legislation...4
       1.1.3   Citing secondary sources 4
       1.1.4   Order of sources in footnotes 5
   1.2   Subsequent citations, cross-references and Latin 'gadgets'.....5
       1.2.1   Subsequent citations..5
       1.2.2   Cross-references...8
       1.2.3   Latin 'gadgets'..8
   1.3   Punctuation, ranges of numbers and years, and foreign words 9
       1.3.1   Punctuation..9
       1.3.2   Ranges of numbers and years 9
       1.3.3   Foreign words 9
   1.4   Citing foreign materials...10
   1.5   Quotations 10
   1.6   Tables and lists of abbreviations 12
       1.6.1   Lists of abbreviations 12
       1.6.2   Order of tables 12
       1.6.3   Tables of cases 12
       1.6.4   Tables of legislation and other tables 13
   1.7   Bibliographies...14
2 Primary Sources 16
   2.1   The Constitution..16
   2.2   Case Law...16
       2.2.1   General principles..16
       2.2.2   Case names 18
       2.2.3   Neutral citations...20
       2.2.4   Law reports...21
       2.2.5   Courts 23
       2.2.6   Pinpoints 23
       2.2.7   Judges' names 23
       2.2.8   Subsequent history of a case 25

2.3 Primary legislation 25
   2.3.1 Names of statutes 25
   2.3.2 Parts of statutes 25
   2.3.3 Older statutes 27
   2.3.4 Explanatory memoranda to statutes 27
   2.3.5 Bills 27
2.4 Secondary legislation 28
   2.4.1 Statutory instruments 28
   2.4.2 Rules of court 28
   2.4.3 Parts of statutory instruments 29
2.5 European Union legal sources 29
   2.5.1 EU legislation 29
   2.5.2 Judgments of the European Court of Justice and General Court 31
   2.5.3 Decisions of the European Commission 32
2.6 The European Court of Human Rights 32
   2.6.1 Judgments of the European Court of Human Rights . 32
   2.6.2 Decisions and reports of the European Commission on Human Rights 33
2.7 Cases and legislation from other jurisdictions 33
   2.7.1 Cases 33
   2.7.2 Legislation 34

3 Secondary sources 35
  3.1 General principles 35
   3.1.1 Authors' names 35
   3.1.2 Titles 35
   3.1.3 Parts, chapters, pages and paragraphs 35
   3.1.4 Electronic sources 35
   3.1.5 Subsequent citations and short forms 36
  3.2 Books 36
   3.2.1 Authored books 36
   3.2.2 Edited and translated books 37
   3.2.3 Contributions to edited books 38
   3.2.4 Older works 38
   3.2.5 Books of authority and institutional works 38
   3.2.6 Encyclopaedias 39
   3.2.7 Looseleaf services 39
  3.3 Articles 40

3.3.1	Hard copy journals	40
3.3.2	Case notes	41
3.3.3	Forthcoming articles	41
3.3.4	Online journals	42
3.3.5	Working papers	42
3.4	Other secondary sources	43
3.4.1	General principles	43
3.4.2	Parliamentary reports	43
3.4.3	Official publications	44
3.4.4	Law Reform Commission Reports and Consultation Papers	45
3.4.5	European Commission documents	45
3.4.6	Conference papers	46
3.4.7	Theses	46
3.4.8	Websites and blogs	46
3.4.9	Newspaper articles	47
3.4.10	Interviews	47
3.4.11	Personal communications	47

Introduction

There are two golden rules for the citation of legal authorities. One is consistency. The other is consideration for the reader. Legal writing is more persuasive when the author refers to legal materials in a clear, consistent and familiar way. When it is easy to identify and to find the author's sources, it becomes easier for the reader to follow the argument. OSCOLA Ireland is designed to help the author to achieve consistency and to make life easier for the reader. OSCOLA Ireland is based on OSCOLA, which was devised by the Faculty of Law at Oxford University.

OSCOLA Ireland does not purport to be comprehensive, but gives rules and examples for the main Irish legal primary sources, and for many types of secondary sources. As far as possible, the guidelines in OSCOLA Ireland are based on common practice in Irish legal citation, but with a minimum of punctuation. When citing materials not mentioned in OSCOLA Ireland, use the general principles in OSCOLA Ireland as a guide, and try to maintain consistency. OSCOLA Ireland is best read in conjunction with OSCOLA.

OSCOLA Ireland is a guide to legal citation, not a style guide. For advice on punctuation, grammar and writing style, use the most recent editions of *Fowler's Modern English Usage*, *The Oxford English Dictionary*, and *Hart's Rules*. *Hart's Rules* is particularly useful for information about typographical conventions, but note that the legal citation section is not always consistent with OSCOLA Ireland.

OSCOLA was originally designed for use within Oxford University, but is now used by law schools throughout the UK and in Ireland, and by a number of legal journals and publishers. Due to the absence of a consistent style guide in Ireland, we sought to adapt and amend OSCOLA to ensure its suitability for Irish students, practitioners and academics. We are, of course, deeply indebted to the editorial team at OSCOLA, and to Donal Nolan and Sandra Meredith in particular. Seth Barrett Tillman at NUI Maynooth provided us with a great deal of useful feedback. We would also like to thank Hugo Kelly, Law Librarian at the National University of Ireland Galway, for his generous assistance with obscure questions of Irish practice.

More information on OSCOLA can be found at law.ox.ac.uk/publications/oscola.php. More information on OSCOLA Ireland can be found at oscola.ie. If you have any comments or suggestions regarding OSCOLA Ireland, please contact us at info@legalcitation.ie.

Larry Donnelly, Elaine Fahey, Rónán Kennedy, and Jennifer Schweppe

February 2016

1 General notes

1.1 Citations and footnotes

When writing for an academic or professional audience, provide evidence for your claims by citing your sources in footnotes. Legal writing cites primary legal sources (cases, statutes and so on), as well as secondary sources such as books, journal articles, websites and policy statements.

OSCOLA Ireland is a footnote style: all citations appear in footnotes. OSCOLA Ireland does not use endnotes or in-text citations, such as '(Brown, 2007)'. Longer works, such as books and theses, also include citations in tables of cases and legislation, and bibliographies.

When citing any source, either directly (as a quotation) or indirectly (by paraphrasing or referring to ideas in a source), cite the reference in a footnote, in the style indicated in OSCOLA Ireland.

Indicate footnotes with a superscript number which should appear after the relevant punctuation in the text (if any). Put the footnote marker at the end of a sentence, unless for the sake of clarity it is necessary to put it directly after the word or phrase to which it relates. If the word or phrase to which the footnote marker relates is in brackets, put the marker before the closing bracket. A quotation need not be footnoted separately from the name of the source from which it is derived if the two appear in the same sentence. Otherwise, separate notes should be used.

Close footnotes with a full stop (or question or exclamation mark). Where more than one citation is given in a single footnote reference, separate them with semi-colons.

1.1.1 Citing cases

When citing cases, give the name of the case, the neutral citation (if appropriate), and volume and first page of the relevant law report, and where necessary the court. If the name of the case is given in the text, it is not necessary to repeat it in the footnote. For example:

> Although Costello J strongly approved of their use in *Wavin Pipes v Hepworth Iron Ltd*,[32] Keane J felt there must be some 'obscurity, ambiguity or potential absurdity in the relevant

provisions which would justify the court having recourse to what was said in the Oireachtas in order to ascertain the legislative intention.'[33] Later, Walsh J stated in *Quilligan* that the search for intention is confined to the text of legislation: 'Whatever may have been in the minds of the members of the Oireachtas when the legislation was passed, in so far as their intention can be deduced ... it must be, from the words of the statute.'[34]

[32] (1982) 8 FSR 32 (HC).

[33] *ACW v Ireland* [1994] 3 IR 232, sub nom *Wadda v Ireland* [1994] 1 ILRM 126 (HC) 137.

[34] *People (DPP) v Quilligan* [1986] IR 495 (SC) 511.

The numbers at the end of footnotes 33 and 34 are called 'pinpoints'; they give the page on which the quotation can be found. It is also acceptable to include the full case reference in all footnotes.

1.1.2 Citing legislation

A citation in a footnote is not required when citing legislation if all the information the reader needs about the source is provided in the text, as in the following sentence:

> This case highlights the limited judicial role provided by the European Convention on Human Rights Act 2003.

Where the text does not include the name of the Act or the relevant section, this information should be provided in a footnote.

> Irish courts must only consider Strasbourg jurisprudence: they are not bound by it.[1]
>
> [1] European Convention on Human Rights Act 2003, s 2.

1.1.3 Citing secondary sources

If relying on or referring to a secondary source, such as a book or an article, provide a citation for the work in a footnote.

> Hart wrote that the doctrine of precedent is compatible with 'two types of creative or legislative activity': *distinguishing* the earlier case by 'narrowing the rule extracted from the precedent', and *widening the rule* by discarding 'a restriction found in the rule as formulated from the earlier case'.[34]

³⁴ HLA Hart, *The Concept of Law* (2nd edn, Clarendon Press 1994) 135.

1.1.4 Order of sources in footnotes

When citing more than one source of the same kind for a single proposition, put the sources in chronological order, with the oldest first. Separate the citations with semi-colons, and do not precede the final citation with 'and'. If one or more of the sources are more directly relevant than the others, cite these first, and then cite the less relevant ones in a new sentence, beginning 'See also'. If citing legislation and case law for a single proposition, put the legislation before the cases, and if citing primary and secondary sources for a single proposition, put the primary sources before the secondary ones.

> ¹ FH Newark, 'The Boundaries of Nuisance' (1949) 65 LQR 480; Richard Kidner, 'Nuisance and Rights of Property' [1998] Conv 267; Ken Oliphant, 'Unblurring the Boundaries of Nuisance' (1998) 6 Tort L Rev 21; Paula Giliker, 'Whither the Tort of Nuisance? The Implications of Restrictions on the Right to Sue in *Hunter v Canary Wharf*' (1999) 7 Torts LJ 155.
>
> ² *Brent v Haddon* (1619) Cro Jac 555, 79 ER 476; *Broder v Saillard* (1876) 2 Ch D 692 (Ch); *Pemberton v Bright* [1960] 1 All ER 792 (CA). See also *Torette House Pty Ltd v Berkman* (1939) 62 CLR 637, 659 (Dixon J).

Further details of how to cite **cases**, **legislation** and **secondary sources** can be found in parts 2 and 3 of OSCOLA Ireland. The appendix to OSCOLA includes **lists of abbreviations** that can be used in footnotes.

1.2 Subsequent citations, cross-references and Latin 'gadgets'

1.2.1 Subsequent citations

In a subsequent citation of a source, briefly identify the source and provide a cross-citation in brackets to the footnote in which the full citation can be found. If the subsequent citation is in the footnote immediately following the full citation, you can generally use 'ibid' instead.

For subsequent citations of cases, a short form of the case name is sufficient to identify the source. Subsequent citations of legislation may use abbreviations or other short forms. Subsequent citations of secondary sources require only the author's or authors' surname(s), unless several works by the same author are being cited, in which case the surname and the title of the work (or a short form of the title) should be given.

Note that it is also acceptable to give the full citation every time a source is cited, and some publishers and law schools may prefer this to the use of short forms. You should always do this if the previous citation was in an earlier chapter.

EXAMPLE of subsequent citation of a case

In this example, a citation for *North Western Health Board v W* is provided in footnote 1. As the name of the case is given in the text, it is not given in the footnote. The second citation at footnote 2 pinpoints several pages in the case with an attribution to the relevant judge in brackets. The third citation at footnote 7 gives a short form of the case name and a cross-citation to the full citation.

> [1] [2001] IESC 90, [2001] 3 IR 622.
>
> [2] ibid 673 (Keane CJ), 712 (Denham J), 738-739 (Murray J), 751-753 (Hardiman J).
>
> ...
>
> [7] *NWHB v W* (n 1).

EXAMPLE of subsequent citation of legislation

This example shows legislation for which a short form could be used in a subsequent citation. The short form is indicated in brackets at the end of the full citation. In such cases, the short form can be used without a cross-citation to the full citation where the proximity of the full citation enables this to be done without confusing the reader. Where that is not the case, a further full citation should be provided, with the result that cross-citation is never necessary.

> [32] Council Directive (EC) 93/104 concerning certain aspects of the organisation of working time [1993] OJ L307/18 (Working Time Directive).
>
> ...
>
> [40] Working Time Directive, art 2.

EXAMPLE of subsequent citation of a book

This example shows a citation of a book which is first cited (in full) at footnote 1, cited again in footnote 26 with a cross-citation to footnote 1, and then cited again at footnote 27.

> [1] James Casey, *Constitutional Law in Ireland* (3rd edn, Round Hall 2000).
>
> ...
>
> [26] Casey (n 1) 110.
>
> [27] ibid 271–78.

EXAMPLE of subsequent citation of two works by the same author

In this example, two different works by the same author are cited. The subsequent citation provides the author's surname and the title of the work, or a short form of the title.

> [27] Andrew Ashworth, 'Testing Fidelity to Legal Values: Official Involvement and Criminal Justice' (2000) 63 MLR 633, 635.
>
> [28] Andrew Ashworth, *Principles of Criminal Law* (6th edn, OUP 2009) 68.
>
> ...
>
> [35] Ashworth, 'Testing Fidelity to Legal Values' (n 27) 635-37.
>
> ...
>
> [46] Ashworth, *Principles of Criminal Law* (n 28) 73.

1.2.2 Cross-references

Cross-references direct the reader to points of substantive discussion elsewhere in your work. Avoid sending the reader off to another part of the text when a short point could as easily be restated. Never make a cross-reference that will be difficult for the reader to find, such as 'See above'. A good cross-reference takes the reader straight to the very place: 'n 109' or, within the same chapter, 'text to n 32'. Do not cross-refer to 'Chapter 6A2(c)' unless you have running headers on each page showing the sequence of sub-headings. Use 'See ...' only when you actually want the reader to look at the place indicated, for example 'See n 109'.

Pagination may change from draft to draft, especially in preparation for publication. It is therefore easiest to cross-refer to footnote markers, for example 'Text to n 107 in ch 7'. Cross-reference functions in word processors can help you keep track of changes in footnote numbers.

1.2.3 Latin 'gadgets'

Avoid the use of 'Latin gadgets' such as *supra*, *infra*, *ante*, *id*, *op cit*, *loc cit*, and *contra*, which are not widely understood. The abbreviation 'ibid', which is short for *ibidem*, meaning 'in the same place', can be used to repeat a citation in the immediately preceding footnote. Standing alone, 'ibid' means strictly 'in the very same place' while 'ibid 345' means 'in the same work, but this time at page 345'. It is equally acceptable to repeat the immediately preceding citation without using 'ibid': 'Ashworth (n 27) 635–37' thus does the trick even in n 28. Do not switch back and forth from one to the other. If there is more than one citation in the preceding footnote, use 'ibid' only if you are referring again to all the citations in that footnote. Note that the abbreviation 'cf' is short for *confer*, meaning 'compare'; it does not mean the same thing as 'see'. Never italicise or capitalise 'ibid' or 'cf'.

> [28] Joseph Raz, *The Authority of Law: Essays on Law and Morality* (2nd edn, OUP 2009).
>
> [29] ibid 6.
>
> ...
>
> [32] cf Raz (n 28) 233–36.

1.3 Punctuation, ranges of numbers and years, and foreign words

1.3.1 Punctuation

OSCOLA Ireland uses as little punctuation as possible. Abbreviations and initials in author's names do not take full stops. For example, *Irish Reports* is cited as 'IR' and the Director of Public Prosecutions is abbreviated to 'DPP'. Insert commas to separate items that may otherwise run together and cause confusion, such as runs of numbers or authors and titles.

> *Riordan v Ireland* [2009] IESC 44, [2009] 3 IR 745
>
> JG Fleming, 'Remoteness and Duty: The Control Devices in Liability for Negligence' (1953) 31 Can Bar Rev 471

When citing authorities from other jurisdictions, do not include full stops in the citation.

1.3.2 Ranges of numbers and years

When referring to ranges of numbers, use both figures for numbers between ten and twenty, and thereafter use as few figures as possible, but always use at least two for the final number.

> 1-6 11-17 21-26 22-32 121-221 1782-83 1782-812

If the range of numbers indicates years, and the years span centuries, give the final year in full.

> 1871-1914 1925-27 1965-75 1989-2001

1.3.3 Foreign words

In the text, italicise words and phrases in languages other than the one you are writing in, but not quotations. Provide a translation immediately afterwards in brackets, or in a footnote, if required. Do not italicise words that are in common usage in legal English, such as ultra vires, stare decisis, obiter dicta, ratio decidendi, a priori and a fortiori. Commonly used abbreviations, such as ie and eg, are not italicised and have no full stops.

1.4 Citing foreign materials

When referring to foreign materials, cite primary sources as in their home jurisdiction, with the exception that full stops in abbreviations should be dropped. Guides for other jurisdictions can be found in section 4.3 of the appendix to OSCOLA. Cite secondary sources in accordance with the OSCOLA Ireland rules governing the citation of secondary sources.

1.5 Quotations

Quotations from other works, cases, statutes and so on must be faithful to the original, except where it is necessary to change quotation marks from single to double, or vice versa. Any comments on the quotation, such as 'emphasis added', should be in a footnote.

Incorporate quotations of up to three lines into the text, within single quotation marks (examples 1 and 2). Quotations within short quotations take double quotation marks. Punctuation follows the closing quotation mark, unless it is an essential part of the quotation, as a question or exclamation mark might be (example 2), or unless the whole sentence is a quotation. The footnote marker comes last, after both the closing quotation mark and the punctuation.

Present quotations longer than three lines in an indented paragraph, with no further indentation of the first line (examples 3 and 4). Do not use quotation marks, except for single quotation marks around quotations within quotations (example 3). Leave a line space either side of the indented quotation.

When a quotation begins in the middle of a sentence in the text, the first letter of the quotation should be capitalised if the quotation itself is a complete sentence, but not otherwise. When a quotation begins at the start of a sentence in the text, the first letter should be capitalised, and square brackets placed around it if it was not capitalised in the original text (example 3). When intervening text is missing from the quotation, or if it ends mid-sentence in the original text, use an ellipsis (…) to indicate that some of the original text is missing. Leave a space between an ellipsis and any text or punctuation, except quotation marks.

If a quotation is incorporated into the text, then no more than a comma (at most) is required to introduce it (examples 1 and 2).

Generally, a colon is used to introduce an indented quotation (example 4).

When it is necessary to attribute a quotation or citation within a quotation to its original source, omit the footnote marker from the original text in your quotation, and give the original author's citation in your footnote (example 3). If it is not necessary to attribute such a quotation or citation because it is either implicit or irrelevant, omit the footnote markers or citations and add '(footnotes omitted)' or '(citations omitted)' after the citation in your own footnote. Similarly, if you add emphasis to a quotation put '(emphasis added)' after the footnote citation (example 4).

EXAMPLE 1
Casey explained that the terms of the Constitution 'show clearly that the President is intended to play a mainly ceremonial role'.[61]

EXAMPLE 2
Bix raises the question, 'What is the point of a dissent, after all, at least on the highest court of the jurisdiction, if the law simply is whatever the majority on that court says it is?'[22]

EXAMPLE 3
[T]he House of Lords also concluded that the civil standard of proof (on the balance of probabilities) should be applied in such a way as to be sensitive to the 'seriousness of the matters to be proved and the implications of proving them', which in effect means proof beyond reasonable doubt (ie the criminal standard).[27]

[27] Andrew Ashworth, 'Social Control and "Anti-Social Behaviour": The Subversion of Human Rights' (2004) 120 LQR 263, 276, citing *Clingham and McCann* [2002] UKHL 39, [2003] 1 AC 787 [83] (Lord Hope).

EXAMPLE 4
Walsh J in *DPP v Quilligan* stated that the search for intention is confined to the text of legislation:

Whatever may have been in the minds of the members of the Oireachtas when the legislation was passed, in so far as

> their intention can be deduced ... *it must be*, from the words of the statute.[12]

[12] [1986] IR 495 (SC) 511 (emphasis added).

1.6 Tables and lists of abbreviations

A longer legal work, such as a book or a thesis, generally has a list of abbreviations and tables of all the cases, legislation and other primary legal sources cited in the work in the preliminary pages. Shorter works, such as articles and essays, generally only require footnotes. Tables should be indexed, so that each entry indicates on what page or pages the primary source in question is mentioned. The list of abbreviations should come before the tables, and the order of the tables should generally be: table of Articles of the Constitution; table of cases; table of legislation; other tables.

1.6.1 Lists of abbreviations

In an article or essay, define unfamiliar abbreviations in a footnote or in the text. In a book or thesis, define unfamiliar abbreviations in a list of abbreviations in the preliminary pages. Do not define abbreviations that are part of everyday legal usage, such as 'DPP'. For lists of common abbreviations that need not be defined, see section 4.2 of the appendix of OSCOLA.

1.6.2 Order of tables

If there is a table of articles of the Constitution, it should come before all other tables, including the table of cases. The table of cases will follow this, or come first if there is no table of articles of the Constitution. Tables of legislation and other tables, such as tables of international treaties and conventions, UN documents, official papers and policy documents, should follow the table of cases.

1.6.3 Tables of cases

In a table of cases, case names are not italicised. Unless there are very few cases, divide the table into separate sections for different jurisdictions. Cases should be listed in alphabetical order of first significant word. Thus, *Re Farquar's Estate* should be tabled as 'Farquar's Estate, Re'. Cases identifying parties by initial only should be listed under the initial, so *Re F (mental patient: sterilisation)* becomes 'F (mental patient: sterilisation), Re'. When listing cases with names such as *DPP v Smith*, or *People (DPP) v Smith* in works on criminal law, drop the 'DPP' (or 'People (DPP)' and list the case as 'Smith', but if citing such cases in a work primarily concerned with another area of law, list them by their full names, under 'DPP' or 'People (DPP), and also do this when citing judicial review cases with the State as the first-named party.

List trade-mark cases and shipping cases under the full case name, but insert an additional entry in the table under the trade mark or the name of the ship (again using the first significant word, so that *The MV Toledo* becomes 'MV Toledo, The'), with a cross-reference to the full name.

> MV Toledo, The. *See* ACT Shipping v Minister for the Marine

If not listed separately, EU cases should be arranged alphabetically by first party name in the table of cases, with the case number following the name of the case in brackets, so that 'Case T–344/99 *Arne Mathisen AS v Council* [2002] ECR II–2905' is cited in the table of cases under 'A' as 'Arne Mathisen AS v Council (T–344/99) [2002] ECR II–2905'. If the table of cases is divided by jurisdiction, list ECJ, CFI and Commission decisions separately, in chronological and numerical order, citing the cases as in footnotes, with the case number first, but omitting the word 'Case'. If a large number of such cases are cited, it may be helpful to compile a separate table of the cases in alphabetical order.

1.6.4   Tables of legislation and other tables

A table of legislation should list every statute cited in the work, with the entry for each statute being sub-divided to show which parts of the statute (sections, sub-sections and so on) are cited where. Statutory instruments should be listed separately, at the end of the list of statutes. If there are a large number of citations of statutory instruments, it may be helpful to have wholly separate tables of statutes and statutory instruments. In tables of legislation, legislation should be listed in alphabetical order of first significant word of the title, not chronologically by date of enactment. If legislation from more than one jurisdiction is cited, it may be helpful to have separate lists for each jurisdiction.

1.7 Bibliographies

In longer works, such as theses and books, a bibliography listing secondary sources should be provided after the main body of text and any appendices. It should include all such sources cited in the work and need not be indexed.

Items in bibliographies take the same form as all other citations in OSCOLA Ireland, with three exceptions: (1) the author's surname should precede his or her initial(s), with no comma separating them, but a comma after the final initial; (2) only initials should be used, and not forenames; and (3) the titles of unattributed works should be preceded by a double em-dash. Works should be arranged in alphabetical order of author surname, with unattributed works being listed at the beginning of the bibliography in alphabetical order of first major word of the title.

CITATION in a footnote

[15] Robert Clark, *Contract Law* (6th edn, Round Hall 2008).

CITATION in a bibliography

Clark R, *Contract Law* (6th edn, Round Hall 2008)

If citing several works by the same author in a bibliography, list the author's works in chronological order (starting with the oldest), and in alphabetical order of first major word of the title within a single year. After the citation of the first work, replace the author's name with a double em-dash. Alphabetise works by more than one author under the first author's name, but place them after that author's sole-authored works. If a first author has more than one co-author, arrange the co-authored works in alphabetical order of co-author surname, and if you are citing more than one work by the same first author and co-author, arrange the works in chronological order, repeating the co-author's name each time.

Hart HLA, Law, Liberty and Morality (OUP 1963)

—— 'Varieties of Responsibility' (1967) 83 LQR 346

—— Punishment and Responsibility (OUP 1968)

—— and Honoré AM, 'Causation in the Law' (1956) 72 LQR 58, 260, 398

—— and Honoré AM, Causation in the Law (2nd edn, OUP 1985)13

2 Primary Sources

2.1 The Constitution

The Irish Constitution, or Bunreacht na hÉireann, should be referred to in the same language as the surrounding text, whether English or Irish. Capitalise Constitution and Article, but not articles (unless referring to a specific set or range) or constitutional. Use a degree symbol ° when referring to a sub-subsection.

> Other articles of the Constitution which protect the rights of the family …
>
> We also find references to the role of the Council of State in Articles 14 and 31.
>
> Article 12.1 states that the President …
>
> The Constitution provides in Article 40.3.3°…

Art (or art) is acceptable as an abbreviation in footnotes:

> [17] Art 40.3.3°.

2.2 Case Law

2.2.1 General principles

The components of a typical case citation are the case name, the neutral citation and the law report. However, neutral citations are a relatively recent development, so many case citations consist only of the case name and the law report. To verify whether a case has a neutral citation, use the website of the Irish Legal Information Institute, www.irlii.org. Most cases decided after 1998 have a neutral citation and some cases have been given retrospective neutral citations.

Use italics for the name of the case, with an unpunctuated italic *v* to separate the names of adverse parties. Use normal text for the rest of the citation. A comma separates the neutral citation and the law report citation. There are no full stops in the abbreviations: hence 'IESC' rather than 'I.E.S.C.' and 'IR' rather than 'I.R.'.

Case citations including neutral citations

The components of a typical case citation including a neutral citation are:

> *case name* | [year] | court | number, | [year] OR (year) | volume | report abbreviation | first page

The example below indicates that the case of *Riordan v Ireland* was the forty-fourth judgment issued by the Supreme Court in 2009, and that a report of the judgment can be found in volume three of the 2009 volume of the *Irish Reports*, beginning at page 745.

> *Riordan v Ireland* [2009] IESC 44, [2009] 3 IR 745

Case citations without neutral citations

The components of a typical case citation without a neutral citation are:

> *case name* | [year] OR (year) | volume | report abbreviation | first page | (court)

As the following example shows, when the year is used to identify the law report volume it is given in square brackets. In such cases, also give a volume number if the series in question was issued in more than one volume during that particular year, but do not do so if only one volume was issued.

> *Ryan v Attorney General* [1965] IR 294 (SC)

Where the year is necessary to identify the volume and there is more than one volume in a year, give the year in square brackets and the volume number before the report abbreviation, as in the following example from volume four of the 1998 *Irish Reports*.

> *Phonographic Performance Ireland Ltd v Cody* [1998] 4 IR 504 (HC)

Give the year of judgment (not publication) in round brackets when the volumes of the law report series are independently numbered, so that the year of publication is not needed to find the volume. For example, a report of *McCarthy v O'Flynn*, which was decided in 1980, can also be found in the one hundred and fourteenth volume of the

Irish Law Times Reports, beginning on page twenty-two. The citation of this report is therefore:

> McCarthy v O'Flynn (1980) 114 ILTR 22 (SC)

2.2.2 Case names

Where there are multiple parties, name only the first claimant and first defendant. Where the parties are individuals, omit forenames and initials. Abbreviate common words and phrases: use *HSE* for *Health Services Executive*, *Co* for *Company*, *DPP* for *Director of Public Prosecutions* and so on (see section **4.2.4** of the appendix of OSCOLA for more abbreviations).

Use *Re* in preference to *In re*, *In the matter of*, and so on: *Re the Companies Act 1963* rather than *In the matter of the Companies Act 1963*, and *Re Farquar's Estate* instead of *In re the Estate of Farquar*. Abbreviate *Ex parte* to *Ex p* with a capital *E* only if it is the first word of the case name. The *p* has no full stop. Do not include expressions such as *and another*, which may appear in titles in law reports. Omit descriptions such as *a firm* if the party in question is named, but if only the initial of the party is provided, then the description (such as *a minor*) should be given, at least in the first citation. Terms indicating corporate status (such as *Ltd* and *plc*) should not be omitted if included in the heading of the report.

> Re A (conjoined twins) [2001] Fam 147
>
> Re Article 26 and the Illegal Immigrants (Trafficking) Bill 1999 [2000] IESC 19, [2000] 2 IR 360
>
> Re Bloomberg Developments Ltd [2002] IESC 56

Short forms of case names

Give the name of the case in full when it is first mentioned in the text or footnotes; it may be shortened thereafter. Thus, 'in *Wavin Pipes v Hepworth Iron Ltd*' can be shortened to 'in the *Wavin Pipes* case' (or 'in *Wavin Pipes*') (example 1). If a case name is shortened in this way, the name chosen must be that which stands first in the full name of the case. In shipping cases, the name of the ship can be used instead of the full case name (example 2). It is common in works on criminal law to see 'in *People (DPP) v Shaw*' shortened to 'in *Shaw*', even in the first citation, but less so where a small number of criminal cases are cited in a work primarily concerned with another area of law. Either form is acceptable (example 3). Popular names for cases may also be used. Give the popular name in brackets after the initial full citation, and then use the popular name in subsequent citations (example 4).

EXAMPLE 1

14 *Wavin Pipes v Hepworth Iron Ltd* (1982) 8 FSR 32.

...

19 *Wavin Pipes* (n 14).

EXAMPLE 2

25 *Leigh & Sillivan Ltd v Aliakmon Shipping Co Ltd (The Aliakmon)* [1986] AC 785 (HL).

...

45 *The Aliakmon* (n 25).

EXAMPLE 3

11 *R v Evans* [2009] EWCA Crim 650, [2009] 1 WLR 13 OR *Evans* [2009] EWCA Crim 650, [2009] 1 WLR 13.

...

23 *R v Evans* (n 11) OR *Evans* (n 11).

EXAMPLE 4

12 *Mirage Studios v Counter-feat Clothing Co Ltd* [1991] FSR 145 (Ch) (Ninja Turtles case).

...

28 Ninja Turtles case (n 12).

Judicial review applications

Before 1986, case names in judicial review applications cited the State against the body under review, on behalf of the individual involved.

The State (Turley) v Ó Floinn [1968] IR 245 (SC)

For cases from 1986 onwards, the following form is used:

Fairleigh v Temple Bar Renewal Ltd [1999] 2 IR 508 (HC)

In both cases, subsequent citations would cite *Turley* or *Fairleigh* in the text or in a footnote.

Variations in the name of a case

Where the same case is reported under significantly different names in different law reports, use the name given in the heading of the report being cited. Where two or more reports using different names are cited, the report or reports using the alternative name of the case should be introduced by the phrase 'sub nom' in roman (an abbreviation of *sub nomine*, meaning 'under the name').

ACW v Ireland [1994] 3 IR 232, sub nom *Wadda v Ireland* [1994] 1 ILRM 126 (HC)

Similarly, where a case appears under a different name at different stages in its history (that difference in the name being more than a mere reversal of the names of the parties), and both stages are being cited, the name of the case at the second stage cited should be introduced by 'sub nom'.

R v Monopolies and Mergers Commission, ex p South Yorkshire Transport Ltd [1992] 1 WLR 291 (CA), affd sub nom *South Yorkshire Transport Ltd v Monopolies and Mergers Commission* [1993] 1 WLR 23 (HL)

2.2.3 Neutral citations

Transcripts of judgments with neutral citations are generally freely available on the Irish Legal Information Institute website (www.irlii.org). Not all judgments have neutral citations. The cases seem to be numbered consecutively through the year. Only some cases with neutral citations have numbered paragraphs – and even within a judgment, some judges will use numbered paragraphs and some will not. If no paragraph numbers are given, do not manually insert them.

Neutral citations give the year of judgment, the court and the judgment number. The court is not included in brackets at the end of a neutral citation because the neutral citation itself identifies the court. Where a judgment with a neutral citation has not been reported, give only the neutral citation, as shown in the last two examples below (note that these judgments may have been reported since OSCOLA Ireland was published). Where such a judgment has been reported, give the neutral citation followed by a citation of the best report, separated by a comma (for information about the 'best report', see section 2.2.4).

> *Gilligan v Special Criminal Court* [2005] IESC 86, [2006] 2 IR 406
>
> *Mahon Tribunal v Keena*[2009] IESC 64, [2009] 2 ILRM 373
>
> *Minister for Justice, Equality & Law Reform v McArdle* [2005] IESC 76
>
> *EMI Records (Ireland) Ltd v Eircom PLC* [2010] IEHC 108

If a single report includes more than one judgment and therefore more than one neutral citation, list the neutral citations in chronological order, starting with the oldest, and separate them with a comma.

> *Masterman-Lister v Brutton & Co (Nos 1 and 2)* [2002] EWCA Civ 1889, [2003] EWCA Civ 70, [2003] 1 WLR 1511

As the unreported judgment is generally available online much earlier than the printed report, it is important to check all neutral citations to see if a report has subsequently become available before finalising your work.

A complete list of neutral citations for the United Kingdom is provided in section 4.1 of the appendix of OSCOLA. For up-to-date information on neutral citation in Ireland, see the case law databases at irlii.org.

2.2.4 Law reports

A law report is a published report of a judgment, with additional features such as a headnote summarising the facts of the case and the judgment, catchwords used for indexing, and lists of cases considered.

The 'best report'

In Ireland, there are no official law reports of any kind, but the *Irish Reports* and the *Irish Law Reports Monthly* are regarded as the most authoritative reports. These reports sometimes include the arguments of counsel.

If a case is reported in one of these two reports, this report should generally be cited in preference to any other report. Where the case is reported in both series, give the *Irish Reports* reference. Only if a judgment is not reported in one of these general series should you refer to another series, such as the *Irish Law Times Reports* or the *Employment Law Reports*.

Heavily edited reports

Where a report of a case gives only a summary or a heavily edited version of the judgment (which is the norm for reports in newspapers and some practitioner journals), cite the report only if there is no neutral citation and no other, fuller, report. When citing a case report, put the title of a newspaper in roman, not italics.

K v K (1998) 2 Irish J Fam L 25 (SC)

Unreported cases

If a case is unreported but has a neutral citation, give that. If an unreported case does not have a neutral citation (which will often be the case before 1998), give the court and the date of the judgment in brackets after the name of the case. There is no need to add the word 'unreported'.

S v Eastern Health Board (HC, 22 July 1988)

Release Speech Therapy v HSE [2011] IEHC 57

Reports using case numbers in the citation

In some specialist law reports, cases are given case numbers which run consecutively through the volumes, rather than page numbers. Examples include the *Reports of Patents Cases*, the *Criminal Appeal Reports* and the *Personal Injuries and Quantum Reports*. In such cases, follow the citation method used by the series in question.

Rozario v Post Office [1997] PIQR P15 (CA)

Thompson Holidays Ltd v Norwegian Cruise Lines Ltd [2002] EWCA Civ 1828, [2003] RPC 32

R v Kelly [2008] EWCA Crim 137, [2008] 2 Cr App R 11

2.2.5 Courts

Indicate the court in brackets after the first page of the report, and before the pinpoint if there is one. Use (SC) for the Supreme Court, (CCA) for the Court of Criminal Appeal, (HC) for the High Court, and (SCC) for the Special Criminal Court. Citations of cases with a neutral citation do not require the court.

2.2.6 Pinpoints

A pinpoint is a reference to a particular paragraph of a judgment or page of a report.

If the judgment has numbered paragraphs, pinpoint to a particular paragraph by putting the relevant paragraph number in square brackets. If the judgment does not have numbered paragraphs and is not available in a form which allows unchanging references (such as a published version, a signed printed transcript or a PDF file), do not provide a pinpoint citation. If pinpointing to more than one paragraph, separate the paragraph numbers in square brackets with a comma. If citing spans of paragraphs, insert a dash between the first and last paragraph being cited.

> *A v Refugee Appeals Tribunal* [2009] IEHC 60 [21], [24]–[25]
>
> *Buckley v A-G* [1950] IR 67 (SC) 82–83

If a law report citation ends with the identification of the court in brackets, the pinpoint follows the closing bracket, without any comma. Where the court is not identified in this way, and you are pinpointing to a page number, insert a comma to prevent the numbers running together. Where the pinpoint reference is to the first page of the report, repeat the page number. Multiple page number pinpoints should be separated by commas.

> *The People (AG) v Bell* [1969] IR 24 (HC) 26, 29
>
> *Hoey v Minister for Justice* [1994] 3 IR 329 (HC) 345–46

2.2.7 Judges' names

Where reference is made to a judge in a case, use the judge's surname followed by the conventional abbreviation identifying their judicial office. Do not use honorifics such as 'the Honourable'.

A High Court or Supreme Court judge is called 'Mr Justice Murphy', or if a woman either 'Mrs Justice Murphy' or 'Ms Justice Murphy', according to her preference (abbreviated 'Murphy J'). To verify the correct form, use the Courts Service web site (courts.ie). Forenames are not used unless there are two judges with the same surname, in which case both the forename and surname of the junior judge of the two is given (for example, 'Roderick Murphy J').

The Chief Justice is abbreviated to 'Murphy CJ', and the name of the President of the High and Circuit and District Courts abbreviated as 'Murphy P'.

Circuit Court judges are referred to as 'His/Her Honour Judge Murphy', with no abbreviation. District Court judges are 'Judge Murphy', with no abbreviation. (Before the coming into force of section 21 of the Courts Act 1991, District Court judges were known as 'justices'.)

If a judge was elevated to a new appointment after the decision in the case you are citing, use the title of the judge at that time; there is no need to add the words 'as he then was'. If referring to more than one judge of the Supreme Court, the High Court, the Court of Criminal Appeal, or the Special Criminal Court in the short form, follow their surnames with JJ. When pinpointing to a particular passage in a judgment, add the judge's name in brackets after the pinpoint. Do not use *per*.

EXAMPLES *in the text*

> Kennedy CJ rejected this argument because ...
>
> This is evident from the decision in *Ryan*, in which Ó Dálaigh CJ said ...
>
> Hardiman and Fennelly JJ were of the opinion that ...
>
> As Lynch J pointed out in ...

EXAMPLES in footnotes

> [101] *Howard v Commissioners of Public Works* [1994] 1 IR 101 (SC) 140 (Finlay CJ); *DPP v McDonagh* [1996] 1 IR 565 (SC) 570 (Costello P); *In re National Irish Bank Ltd* [1999] 3 IR 145 (HC) 164 (Shanley J); *An Blascaod Mór Teo v Commissioners of Public Works (No 2)* [2000] 1 IR 1 (HC) 4 (Budd J).

2.2.8 Subsequent history of a case

The subsequent history of a case may be indicated after the primary citation by abbreviating 'affirmed' to 'affd' and 'reversed' to 'revd'. These abbreviations refer to the decision in the primary citation.

> Ó Beoláin v Fahy [1999] IEHC 161, revd [2001] IESC 37, [2001] 2 IR 279

2.3 Primary legislation
2.3.1 Names of statutes

Cite an Act by its short title and year in normal text, using capitals for the major words, and without a comma before the year.

> Interpretation Act 2005
>
> European Convention on Human Rights Act 2003

If you are referring to a particular Act a number of times in short succession, it is usually possible to use an abbreviated form of the title in the footnotes, without a cross-citation, provided the reader has been warned in advance. The abbreviation is usually the initials of the main words in the title, and should always include the year (so that, for example, the Criminal Justice Act 2006 becomes 'CJA 2006' and not just 'CJA'). In the text, it is acceptable in such circumstances to refer without any prior warning to 'the 2006 Act', but only where this short form is sure to be understood.

> [12] Criminal Procedure Act 1993 (CPA 1993) s 3(1).
>
> ...
>
> [15] CPA 1993, s 2(1)(a)(ii).

If several jurisdictions are discussed in a work, it may be necessary to add the jurisdiction of the legislation in brackets at the end of the citation.

> Civil Liability Act 1961 (Irl)

2.3.2 Parts of statutes

Statutes are divided into parts, sections, subsections, paragraphs and subparagraphs. In addition, the main text of the statute may be supplemented by schedules, which are divided into paragraphs and subparagraphs. The relevant abbreviations are:

part/parts	pt/pts
section/sections	s/ss
subsection/subsections	sub-s/sub-ss
paragraph/paragraphs	para/paras
subparagraph/subparagraphs	subpara/subparas
schedule/schedules	sch/schs

Use the full form at the beginning of a sentence, or when referring to a part of a statute without repeating the name of the Act. Elsewhere in the text, either form can be used, though when referring to subsections or paragraphs it is conventional to use the short form. Use the short form in footnotes. In footnote citation of parts of Acts, insert a comma after the year, and a space but no full stop between the abbreviation and the initial number, letter or opening bracket .

> Sale of Goods and Supply of Services Act 1980, s 2

If specifying a paragraph or subsection as part of a section, use only the abbreviation for the section. For example, paragraph (a) of subsection (2) of section 5 of the European Convention on Human Rights Act 2003 is expressed as follows.

> European Convention on Human Rights Act 2003, s 5(2)(a)

EXAMPLES in the text

> ... section 4(1)(a) of the Criminal Law (Insanity) Act 2006 ... OR ... the Criminal Law (Insanity) Act, s 4(1)(a) ...
>
> ... by virtue of section 2(1)(b)(i) of the Prohibition of Incitement to Hatred Act 1989...
>
> ... as provided by sections 1(2) and 7(2) ...
>
> Subsection (1) does not apply to ...
>
> ... as sub-s (3) shows ...

EXAMPLES in footnotes

[34] Planning and Development (Strategic Infrastructure) Act 2006, ss 32(1) and 157(1).

[35] Sustainable Energy Act 2002, s 6(c).

2.3.3 Older statutes

For older statutes, it may be helpful to give the regnal year and chapter number.

> Crown Debts Act 1801 (41 Geo 3 c 90)

In this example, the information in brackets indicates that the Act was given royal assent in the forty-first year of the reign of George III. The abbreviation c stands for chapter. The Crown Debts Act 1801 was the ninetieth Act to receive royal assent in that session of Parliament, and so is chapter 90. Citation by chapter number must be used for older statutes without short titles.

2.3.4 Explanatory memoranda to statutes

When citing explanatory memoranda to statutes, precede the name of the statute with the words 'Explanatory Memorandum to the …'. As the explanatory memorandum is attached to the Bill rather than to the Act, ensure that you refer to the Bill, followed by the full title of the enacted legislation. When pinpointing, cite the page number(s).

> Explanatory Memorandum to the Student Support Bill 2008 (Student Support Act 2011), 3.

2.3.5 Bills

Cite a Bill by its title, the house in which it originated, the year of presentation, and the number assigned to it. When a Bill is reprinted at any stage it is given a new number.

> title | Dáil Bill | number OR title | Seanad Bill | Year | number

The rules for referring to parts of Bills mirror those for referring to parts of statutes (see section 2). 'Clause' and 'clauses' may be abbreviated to 'cl' and 'cls' in the text and should be so abbreviated in footnotes.

> Communications Regulation (Postal Services) Seanad Bill (2010) 50

Planning and Development (Amendment) (No 3) Dáil Bill (2004) 49, cl 4

2.4 Secondary legislation

2.4.1 Statutory instruments

Statutory instruments (orders, regulations or rules) are numbered consecutively throughout the year. The year combines with the serial number to provide an SI number that follows the abbreviation 'SI' and which is used to identify the legislation. Before the Statutory Instruments Act 1947, secondary legislation in Ireland was known as statutory rules and orders, for which the abbreviation SR&O should be used. When citing a statutory instrument, give the name, year and (after a comma) the SI number.

Planning and Development Regulations 2008, SI 2008/235

National School Teachers' Superannuation Scheme 1934, SR&O 1934/23

As with statutes (see section 2.3.1), where the same statutory instrument is cited a number of times in the same work, an abbreviated form can be used in the footnotes (such as 'EPB 2006' for the European Communities (Energy Performance Of Buildings) Regulations 2006), provided due warning is given with the first full citation .

2.4.2 Rules of court

The Rules of the Superior Courts (RSC), the Rules of the Circuit Court (RCC) and the Rules of the District Court (RDC) may be cited without reference to their SI number or year. Rules of court are divided into Orders (Ord) and rules (r). Cite all other court rules in full as statutory instruments.

RSC Ord 27, r 9

RCC Ord 15, r 2

Practice Directions (PD) are referred to simply by number, as listed on the Courts Service web site.

PD HC48

PD CC01

2.4.3 Parts of statutory instruments

The rules for referring to parts of statutory instruments mirror those for referring to parts of statutes (see section 2) . As with statutes, in the text use the full form at the start of a sentence, and either the full or abbreviated form elsewhere. Use the short form in footnotes. In addition to those given above for parts of statutes, use the following abbreviations:

regulation/regulations	reg/regs
rule/rules	r/rr
article/articles	art/arts

When referring to parts of the rules of court, do not insert a comma before the pinpoint.

European Communities (Greenhouse Gas Emissions Trading) Regulations 2004, SI 2004/437, art 4

2.5 European Union legal sources

Official notices of the EU are carried in the *Official Journal of the European Communities* (abbreviated to OJ). The OJ citation is given in the order: year, OJ series, number/page. The letter 'L' denotes the legislation series (the 'C' series contains EU information and notices, and the 'S' series invitations to tender).

2.5.1 EU legislation

When citing EU treaties and protocols, give the title of the legislation, including amendments if necessary, followed by the year of publication, the OJ series and the issue and page numbers. Older treaties were published in the C series. With notable exceptions, such as the Lisbon Treaty, legislation is now published in the L series.

| legislation title | [year] | OJ series | issue/first page |

> Protocol to the Agreement on the Member States that do not fully apply the Schengen acquis—Joint Declarations [2007] OJ L129/35
>
> Consolidated Version of the Treaty on European Union [2008] OJ C115/13

Cite Regulations, Directives, Decisions, Recommendations and Opinions by giving the legislation type, number and title, followed by publication details in the OJ. Note that the year precedes the running number in citations to Directives, but follows it in citations to Regulations.

> legislation type | number | title | [year] | OJ L issue/first page

> Council Directive 2002/60/EC of 27 June 2002 laying down specific provisions for the control of African swine fever and amending Directive 92/119/EEC as regards Teschen disease and African swine fever [2002] OJ L192/27
>
> Council Regulation (EC) 1984/2003 of 8 April 2003 introducing a system for the statistical monitoring of trade in bluefin tuna, swordfish and big eye tuna within the Community [2003] OJ L295/1

Short forms and pinpoints

Give EU legislation its full name on first citation. In subsequent citations, a short form of the title may be used (provided warning is given in the first citation) and in a footnote you may also just give the document type and number (using 'Reg' and 'Dir' as abbreviations). Pinpoints indicating articles (abbreviated 'art' or 'arts') or paragraphs follow the OJ citation and a comma. For more information about subsequent citations, see section 1.2.1.

Older EU legislation

For the years 1952–72 (when there was no English edition of the *Journal Officiel*), refer where possible to the Special Edition of the OJ.

> Council Regulation (EEC) 1017/68 applying rules of competition to transport by rail, road and inland waterway [1968] OJ Spec Ed 302

2.5.2 Judgments of the European Court of Justice and General Court

Since 1989, EU cases have been numbered according to whether they were registered at the European Court of Justice (ECJ) or the General Court(GC), and given the prefix C– (for ECJ cases) or T– (for GC cases). The General Court was called the Court of First Instance (CFI) until 2009. Judgments from the Civil Service Tribunal, which was established in 2005, are prefixed F–. Do not add a C– to pre-1989 cases.

Give the case registration number in roman and then the name of the case in italics, with no punctuation between them. Give the report citation in the same form as for Irish cases .

> case number | *case name* | [year] | report abbreviation | first page

Where possible, refer to the official reports, which are cited as ECR. ECJ cases are reported in volume one (ECR I–) and GC cases are reported in volume two (ECR II–). The volume number, which is in roman numerals, attaches to the page number with a dash . If an ECR reference is not available, the second best report is usually the *Common Market Law Reports* (CMLR).

For an unreported case, cite the relevant notice in the OJ. If the case is not yet reported in the OJ, then cite the case number and case name, followed by the court and date of judgment in brackets . (Please note that unreported cases given here as examples will have been reported subsequently .)

> Case 240/83 *Procureur de la République v ADBHU* [1985] ECR 531
>
> Joined Cases C-430 and 431/93 *Jereon van Schijndel v Stichting Pensioenfonds voor Fysiotherapeuten* [1995] ECR I-4705
>
> Case T-344/99 *Arne Mathisen AS v Council* [2002] ECR II-2905
>
> Case C-556/07 *Commission v France* [2009] OJ C102/8
>
> Case T-277/08 *Bayer Healthcare v OHMI—Uriach Aquilea* OTC (CFI, 11 November 2009)

When pinpointing, use 'para' or 'paras' after a comma.

> Case C-176/03 *Commission v Council* [2005] ECR I-7879, paras 47-48

Opinions of Advocates General

When citing an opinion of an Advocate General, add the words 'Opinion of AG [name]' after the case citation and a comma, and before any pinpoint.

> Case C-411/05 *Palacios de la Villa v Cortefiel Servicios SA* [2007] ECR I-8531, Opinion of AG Mazák, paras 79-100

2.5.3 Decisions of the European Commission

Decisions of the European Commission in relation to competition law and mergers are to be treated as cases. Give the names of the parties (or the commonly used short name) in italics, the case number in brackets, the Commission Decision number (where available), and the OJ report.

> *case name* | (case number) | Commission Decision number | [year] | OJ L issue/first page

> *Alcatel/Telettra* (Case IV/M.042) Commission Decision 91/251/EEC [1991] OJ L122/48

> *Georg Verkehrsorgani v Ferrovie dello Stato* (Case COMP/37.685) Commission Decision 2004/33/EC [2004] OJ L11/17

2.6 The European Court of Human Rights

2.6.1 Judgments of the European Court of Human Rights

For judgments of the European Court of Human Rights (ECtHR), cite either the official reports, the *Reports of Judgments and Decisions* (cited as ECHR) or the *European Human Rights Reports* (EHRR), but be consistent in your practice. Before 1996, the official reports were known as Series A and numbered consecutively. The EHRR series is also numbered consecutively, but from 2001 case numbers have been used instead of page numbers.

References to unreported judgments should give the application number, and then the court and the date of the judgment in brackets. When pinpointing, use 'para' or 'paras' after a comma. Further information can be obtained from the ECHR website and the HUDOC database at www.echr.coe.int.

Johnston v Ireland (1986) Series A no 122

Osman v UK ECHR 1998-VIII 3124

Balogh v Hungary App no 47940/99 (ECtHR, 20 July 2004)

Omojudi v UK (2010) 51 EHRR 10

2.6.2 Decisions and reports of the European Commission on Human Rights

Citations of decisions and reports of the European Commission on Human Rights, which ceased to function in 1998, should give the year of the decision in brackets, and then refer to the *Decisions and Reports* of the Commission (DR), or, for decisions prior to 1974, to the *Collection of Decisions* of the Commission (CD). If available, a reference to a report of the decision in the EHRR is also acceptable, but if citing the EHRR for a decision of the Commission insert '(Commission Decision)' after the rest of the citation. If the decision is unreported, give the application number, and then in brackets 'Commission Decision' and the date of the decision.

X v Netherlands (1971) 38 CD 9

Council of Civil Service Unions v UK (1987) 10 EHRR 269 (Commission Decision)

Simpson v UK (1989) 64 DR 188

P v UK App no 13473/87 (Commission Decision, 11 July 1988)

2.7 Cases and legislation from other jurisdictions

2.7.1 Cases

Cite cases from other jurisdictions as they are cited in their own jurisdiction, but with minimal punctuation. If the name of the law report series cited does not itself indicate the court, and the identity of the court is not obvious from the context, you should also give this in either full or short form in brackets at the end of the citation. When citing a decision of the highest court of a US state, the abbreviation of the name of the state suffices.

> *Austin v Commissioner of Police for the Metropolis* [2009] UKHL 5, [2009] AC 564
>
> *Henningsen v Bloomfield Motors Inc* 161 A 2d 69 (NJ 1960)
>
> *Roe v Wade* 410 US 113 (1973)
>
> *Waltons Stores (Interstate) Ltd v Maher* (1988) 164 CLR 387
>
> BGH NJW 1992, 1659
>
> Cass civ (1) 21 January 2003, D 2003, 693
>
> CA Colmar 25 January 1963, Gaz Pal 1963.I.277

2.7.2 Legislation

Cite legislation from other jurisdictions as it is cited in its own jurisdiction, but without any full stops in abbreviations. Give the jurisdiction if necessary.

> Human Rights Act 1998 (UK)
>
> Accident Compensation Act 1972 (NZ)
>
> 1976 Standard Terms Act (*Gesetz über Allgemeine Geschäftsbedingungen*) (FRG)
>
> *loi* n° 75-1349 du 31 décembre 1975 relative à l'emploi de la langue française

Guides for citations from other jurisdictions can be found in section 4.3 of the appendix of OSCOLA.

3 Secondary sources

3.1 General principles

3.1.1 Authors' names

Give the author's name exactly as it appears in the publication, but omit postnominals such as SC. When judges write extra-curially, they should be named as in the publication in question. If there are more than three authors, give the name of the first author followed by 'and others' . If no individual author is identified, but an organisation or institution claims editorial responsibility for the work, then cite it as the author. If no person, organisation or institution claims responsibility for the work, begin the citation with the title. Treat editors' names in the same way as authors' names.

In footnotes, the author's first name or initial(s) precede their surname. In bibliographies, the surname comes first, then the initial(s), followed by a comma (see section 1.7) .

3.1.2 Titles

Italicise titles of books and similar publications, including all publications with ISBNs. All other titles should be within single quotation marks and in roma . Capitalise the first letter in all major words in a title. Minor words, such as 'for', 'and', 'or' and 'the', do not take a capital unless they begin the title or subtitle.

3.1.3 Parts, chapters, pages and paragraphs

Pinpoints to parts, chapters, pages and paragraphs come at the end of the citation. Use 'pt' for part, 'ch' for chapter, and 'para' for paragraph. Page numbers stand alone, without 'p' or 'pp'. If citing a chapter or part and page number, insert a comma before the page number. Where possible, give a specific range of pages but if you must refer to an initial page and several unspecified following pages, give the initial page number followed immediately by 'ff' (eg '167ff').

3.1.4 Electronic sources

If you source a publication online which is also available in hard copy, cite the hard copy version . There is no need to cite an electronic source for such a publication.

Citations of publications that are available only electronically should end with the web address (Uniform Resouce Locator or 'url') in angled brackets (< >), followed by the date of most recent access, expressed in the form 'accessed 1 January 2011' . Include 'http://' only if the web address does not begin with 'www'. More detailed guidelines for the citation of electronic sources can be found in sections 3.3.4, 3.3.5 and 3.4.8.

3.1.5 Subsequent citations and short forms

In subsequent citations of books and articles, cite only the author's surname and provide a cross-citation (in the form (n *n*)) to the footnote with the full citation. The pinpoint follows the cross-citation. If you cite more than one work by the same author, it may be useful to provide the title as well, or a short form thereof, and the title alone should be used in subsequent citations of unattributed works and some other secondary sources, such as reports and policy documents. Further advice on subsequent citations and short forms is given in section 1.2.

3.2 Books

Cite all publications with an ISBN as if they were books, whether read online or in hard copy. Older books do not have ISBNs, but should be cited as books even if read online.

3.2.1 Authored books

Cite the author's name first, followed by a comma, and then the title of the book in italics (see section 3.1). Where a book has a title and subtitle not separated with punctuation, insert a colon. Publication information follows the title within brackets . Publication elements should always include the publisher and the year of publication, with a space but no punctuation between them . The place of publication need not be given . If you are citing an edition other than the first edition, indicate that using the form '2nd edn' (or 'rev edn' for a revised edition). Additional information should be of a clarifying nature: it may include the editor, the translator or other descriptive information about the work .

| author, | *title* | (additional information, | edition, | publisher | year) |

> Kerry O'Halloran, *Adoption Law and Practice* (Round Hall 2010)
>
> Gerard Hogan and Gerry Whyte, *Kelly: The Irish Constitution* (4th edn, Butterworths 2003)

If a book consists of more than one volume, the volume number follows the publication details, unless the publication details of the volumes vary, in which case it precedes them, and is separated from the title by a comma. Pinpoint to paragraphs rather than pages if the paragraphs are numbered.

> Christian von Bar, *The Common European Law of Torts*, vol 2 (CH Beck 2000) para 76
>
> Eoin Quill, *Torts in Ireland* (3rd edn, Gill and MacMillan 2009) 125
>
> Julian V Roberts and Mike Hough, *Public Opinion and the Jury: An International Literature Review* (Ministry of Justice Research Series 1/09, 2009) 42

3.2.2 Edited and translated books

If there is no author, cite the editor or translator as you would an author, adding in brackets after their name '(ed)' or '(tr)', or '(eds)' or '(trs)' if there is more than one.

> Ursula Kilkelly (ed), *The ECHR and Irish Law* (2nd edn, Jordans 2009)
>
> Peter Birks and Grant McLeod (trs), *The Institutes of Justinian* (Duckworth 1987)

If the work has an author, but an editor or translator is also acknowledged on the front cover, cite the author in the usual way and attribute the editor or translator at the beginning of the publication information, within the brackets.

> HLA Hart, *Punishment and Responsibility: Essays in the Philosophy of Law* (John Gardner ed, 2nd edn, OUP 2008)
>
> K Zweigert and H Kötz, *An Introduction to Comparative Law* (Tony Weir tr, 3rd edn, OUP 1998)

3.2.3 Contributions to edited books

When citing a chapter or essay in an edited book, cite the author and the title of the contribution, in a similar format to that used when citing an article, and then give the editor's name, the title of the book in italics, and the publication information . It is not necessary to give the pages of the contribution.

> author, | 'title' | in editor (ed), | *book title* | (additional information, | publisher | year)

Justine Pila, 'The Value of Authorship in the Digital Environment' in William H Dutton and Paul W Jeffreys (eds), *World Wide Research: Reshaping the Sciences and Humanities in the Century of Information* (MIT Press 2010)

John Cartwright, 'The Fiction of the "Reasonable Man"' in AG Castermans and others (eds), *Ex Libris Hans Nieuwenhuis* (Kluwer 2009)

3.2.4 Older works

Books published before 1800 commonly have as 'publisher' a long list of booksellers; in such cases it is appropriate to cite merely the date and place of publication . When citing a recent publication of an older work, it may be appropriate to indicate the original publication date within the brackets and before the publication details of the recent publication.

Thomas Hobbes, *Leviathan* (first published 1651, Penguin 1985) 268

3.2.5 Books of authority and institutional works

A small number of older works, such as Blackstone's Commentaries, are regarded as books of authority, and are therefore generally accepted as reliable statements of the law of their time. These works have evolved commonly known abbreviations and citation forms, which should be used in all footnote references to them. A list of some of these works and their abbreviations can be found in section 4.2.3 of the appendix of OSCOLA.

3 Bl Comm 264

Co Litt 135a

3.2.6 Encyclopaedias

Cite an encyclopedia much as you would a book, but excluding the author or editor and publisher and including the edition and year of issue or reissue. Pinpoints to volumes and paragraphs come after the publication information. When an encyclopaedia credits an author for a segment, give both the author and the segment title at the beginning of the citation. If citing an online encyclopedia, give the web address and date of access .

Halsbury's Laws (5th edn, 2010) vol 57, para 53

CJ Friedrich, 'Constitutions and Constitutionalism', *International Encyclopedia of the Social Sciences III* (1968) 319

Leslie Green, 'Legal Positivism', *The Stanford Encyclopedia of Philosophy* (Fall edn, 2009) <http://plato .stanford .edu/archives/fall2009/entries/legal-positivism> accessed 20 November 2009

3.2.7 Looseleaf services

For looseleaf services, cite the title of the work in italics, excluding the name of the current author or editor, but including names which have become part of the title. Do not give publication details. Try to avoid pinpointing when referring to looseleafs, but if you must do so give the volume (if appropriate), and pinpoint to paragraphs rather than pages . If pinpointing, you should also give the release number and/or date of issue at the foot of the relevant page in brackets after the paragraph number, in the form used by the publisher, but without any full stops.

Irish Current Law Statues Annotated 1997-1998, para 15-15 (R 62 August 1998)

Irish Copyright and Design Law, paras 25-30 (Issue 6)

Consolidated Company Legislation, para A-354 (R 5 April 2008)

3.3 Articles

3.3.1 Hard copy journals

When citing articles, give the author's name as given first, followed by a comma. Then give the title of the article, in roman within single quotation marks. After the title, give the publication information in the following order:

• year of publication, in square brackets if it identifies the volume, in round brackets if there is a separate volume number;

• the volume number if there is one (include an issue number if the page numbers begin again for each issue within a volume, which is common for Irish journals, in which case put the issue number in brackets immediately after the volume number);

• the name of the journal in roman, in full or abbreviated form, with no full stops;

and

• the first page of the article.

author,	'title'	[year]	journal name or abbreviation	first page of article
[OR]
author,	'title'	(year)	volume	journal name or abbreviation	first page of article

For guidance on journal abbreviations, see section 4.2.1 of the appendix of OSCOLA.

Abbreviations do vary, so choose an abbreviation and stick with it throughout your work. Some publishers prefer all journal names to be given in full.

Some Irish publications, notably the Irish Jurist, the Dublin University Law Journal and the Irish Law Times (formerly the Irish Law Times and Reports) have been re-launched in recent decades. These so-called 'new series' re-started their volume numbering when they began publishing afresh in 1966, 1978 and 1981 respectively, and citations to issues of these journals since these dates should contain the abbreviation '(ns)' (short for new series) in order to avoid confusion with the previous publication run. Citations to the older series should omit this abbreviation.

> Siobhán Mullally, 'Searching for Foundations for Irish Constitutional Law' (1998) 33 IJ (ns) 333
>
> G F Whyte, 'Natural Law and the Constitution' (1996) 14 ILT (ns) 8
>
> VTH Delany, 'Injuries to Schoolchildren: The Principles of Liability' (1962-63) IJ 15

For journals other than those with a new series, you should use the following to cite articles. Put a comma after the first page of the article if there is a pinpoint.

> Terence Coghlan, 'The Copyright and Related Rights Act 2000' (2001) 6 Bar Review 294
>
> Sally Wheeler and Gary Wilson, 'Corporate Law Firms and the Spirit of Community' (1998) 49 NILQ 239, 239

3.3.2 Case notes

Treat case notes with titles as if they were journal articles. Where there is no title, use the name of the case in italics instead, and add (note) at the end of the citation.

> Andrew Ashworth, '*R (Singh) v Chief Constable of the West Midlands Police*' [2006] Crim LR 441 (note)

If the case discussed in the note is identified in the text it is not necessary to put the name of the case in the case-note citation as well. In such a case, the example above would become:

> Andrew Ashworth [2006] Crim LR 441 (note)

Even if not separately cited, the case should be included in the table of cases, citing its best report.

3.3.3 Forthcoming articles

Cite forthcoming articles in the same way as published articles, following the citation with '(forthcoming)'. If volume and/or page numbers are not yet known, simply omit that information.

3.3.4 Online journals

When citing journal articles which have been published only electronically, give publication details as for articles in hard copy journals, but note that online journals may lack some of the publication elements (for example, many do not include page numbers). If citation advice is provided by the online journal, follow it, removing full stops as necessary to comply with OSCOLA Ireland. Follow the citation with the web address (in angled brackets) and the date you most recently accessed the article. Pinpoints follow the citation and come before the web address.

| author, | 'title' | [year] OR (year) | volume/issue | journal name or abbreviation | <web address> | date accessed |

Graham Greenleaf, 'The Global Development of Free Access to Legal Information' (2010) 1(1) EJLT <http://ejlt.org/article/view/17> accessed 27 July 2010

James Boyle, 'A Manifesto on WIPO and the Future of Intellectual Property' 2004 Duke L & Tech Rev 0009 <www.law.duke.edu/journals/dltr/articles/2004dltr0009.html> accessed 18 November 2009

Citation guidelines for other electronic works are provided in section 3.4.8.

3.3.5 Working papers

Working papers may be available online on institution websites and on sites such as the Social Science Research Network (www.ssrn.com). They should be cited in a similar fashion to electronic journal articles. Because the content of working papers is subject to change, the date of access is particularly important. If a working paper is subsequently published in a journal, cite that in preference to the working paper.

John M Finnis, 'On Public Reason' (2006) Oxford Legal Studies Research Paper 1/2007, 8 <http://ssrn.com/abstract=955815> accessed 18 November 2009

3.4 Other secondary sources
3.4.1 General principles
Follow the general principles for citing secondary sources (section 3.1). If a source has an ISBN, cite it like a book. Generally, cite sources that do not have ISBNs in a similar way, but with the title in roman and within single quotation marks, as for journal articles.

> author, | 'title' | (additional information, | publisher | year)

Additional information may include a document number, a document description, a date of adoption and any other information that may help a reader to locate the source. The publisher may be a government body or an organisation, and it is also possible that no publisher will be identifiable. Depending on the source, it may be more appropriate to provide the publication date, rather than the year. If a source is available only online, then give the web address and the date of access as described in section 3.1.4.

If you wish to use an abbreviated name for the source in subsequent citations, give the short form in brackets at the end of the first citation.

> University of Oxford, *Report of Commission of Inquiry* (OUP 1966) vol 1, ch 3 (Franks Report)
>
> Simon Whittaker, 'La Protection du Consommateur Contre les Clauses Abusives en Grande Bretagne' (Commission des Clauses Abusives 2009) <www.clauses-abusives.fr/colloque/swhittaker.htm> accessed 19 November 2009
>
> Lord Bingham, 'Keynote Address' (Liberty conference, London, 6 June 2009) <www.liberty-human-rights.org.uk/publications/3-articles-and-speeches/index.shtml> accessed 19 November 2009

3.4.2 Parliamentary reports
The Official Reports of the Oireachtas are in three series, one reporting debates on the floor of the Dáil, one reporting debates on the floor of the Seanad and one reporting debates in Oireachtas committees.

When referring to the first two series, cite the house followed by 'Deb', then the full date, the volume and the column . Use 'col' or 'cols' for column(s).

| Dáil Deb OR Seanad Deb | date, | volume, | column |

Dáil Deb 5 October 2005, vol 606, col 1690

Cite debates in Oireachtas committees with the name of the committee, followed by 'Deb', followed by the date and page number.

Select Committee on Enterprise and Small Business Deb 30 June 1998, 3

Special Committee Wildlife Bill, 1975 Deb 1 July 1976, 4

When citing reports of select committees of either house, or joint committees of both houses, give the name of the committee, the title of the report in italics, and then in brackets the document number, which should begin with P, followed by the year of publication, if available and clear. (Not all committee reports carry a publication date. This can sometimes be determined from other sources but it is best not to guess.)

Joint Committee on Climate Change and Energy Security, *Second Report On Climate Change Law* (Prn A10/1448, 2010)

Committee of Public Accounts, *Third Interim Report on the Procurement of Legal Services by Public Bodies* (Prn A11/0171, 2011)

Select Committee on Crime, Lawlessness and Vandalism, *Fifteenth Report: The Prosecution of Offences* (PL 4703, 1987) 11

Sub-Committee of the Committee on Procedure and Privileges, *First Report on Reform of Dáil Procedure* (Pn 2814, 1996) 29

3.4.3   Official publications

Official publications include White and Green Papers, relevant treaties, government responses to joint committee reports, and reports of committees of inquiry. When citing an official publication, begin the citation with the name of the department or other body that produced the document, and then give the title of the paper in italics, followed by the document number (if available) and the year in brackets. If additional information is required, insert it within the brackets before the document number.

The abbreviation preceding a document number should begin with P, is usually Prn, Pn or Prl and indicates that the document was laid before the Houses of the Oireachtas.

> All-Party Oireachtas Committee on the Constitution, *Bunreacht na hÉireann: A Study of the Irish Text* (Pn 7899, 1999) 286
>
> Tribunal of Inquiry into Certain Planning Matters and Payments, *Second Interim Report* (2002) 66
>
> Working Group on the Jurisdiction of the Courts, *The Criminal Jurisdiction of the Courts* (Pn 237, 2003) ch 4

3.4.4 Law Reform Commission Reports and Consultation Papers

Cite Law Reform Commission reports by title in italics, Commission number and year, separated by an em dash. For Law Reform Commission consultation papers, give the LRC CP number.

> Law Reform Commission, *Report on Privity of Contract and Third Party Rights* (LRC 88—2008)
>
> Law Reform Commission, *Consultation Paper on Legal Aspects of Family Relationships* (LRC CP 55—2009)

3.4.5 European Commission documents

When citing European Commission documents (such as proposals and action plans), give the body that produced the document, followed by the title in quotation marks, and the COM number. Describe the document type in brackets after the title if appropriate. In subsequent citations give only the COM number.

> Commission, 'Proposal for a Council Decision on the conclusion, on behalf of the European Community, of the Protocol on the Implementation of the Alpine Convention in the Field of Transport (Transport Protocol)' COM (2008) 895 final, ch I, art 3

Commission, 'Action Plan on consumer access to justice and the settlement of disputes in the internal market' (Communication) COM (96) 13 final

Commission, 'Proposal for a Council Regulation on jurisdiction and the recognition and enforcement of judgments in civil and commercial matters' COM (99) 348 final

3.4.6 Conference papers

When citing conference papers that were only available at a conference or directly from the author, give the author, the title in quotation marks and then in brackets the title, location and date of the conference. If a conference paper has been published, cite the published version instead; papers that are available online should include a web address and date of access. Cite conference papers that are not publicly available only if you have the author's permission.

> Ben McFarlane and Donal Nolan, 'Remedying Reliance: The Future Development of Promissory and Proprietary Estoppel in English Law' (Obligations III conference, Brisbane, July 2006)

3.4.7 Theses

When citing an unpublished thesis, give the author, the title and then in brackets the type of thesis, university and year of completion.

> Javan Herberg, 'Injunctive Relief for Wrongful Termination of Employment' (DPhil thesis, University of Oxford 1989)

3.4.8 Websites and blogs

Where there is no relevant advice elsewhere in OSCOLA, follow the general principles for secondary sources (section 3.1) when citing websites and blogs. If there is no author identified, and it is appropriate to cite an anonymous source, begin the citation with the title in the usual way . If there is no date of publication on the website, give only the date of access.

> Fiona de Londras, 'Adjudication, Constitutionalism and Trying to "Save" the ECHR' (*Human Rights in Ireland*, 26 January 2011) <www.humanrights.ie/index.php/2011/01/26/adjudication-constitutionalism-and-trying-to-save-the-ecthr> accessed 30 January 2011

3.4.9 Newspaper articles

When citing newspaper articles, give the author, the title, the name of the newspaper in italics and then in brackets the city of publication and the date. Some newspapers have 'The' in the title and some do not. If known, give the number of the page on which the article was published, after the brackets. If the newspaper is divided into sections, and the page numbering begins afresh in each section, put the section name in roman before the page number, with a space but no comma between the two. If the reference is to an editorial, cite the author as 'Editorial'. If the article is sourced from the web and there is no page number available, provide the web address and date of access.

> Carl O'Brien, 'Woman with Cancer Tells of her Abortion Ordeal' *The Irish Times* (Dublin, 21 December 2010)
>
> Shane Phelan and Tim Healy, 'Top Anglo Chiefs are Blocking Garda Probe' *Irish Independent* (Dublin, 5 May 2011)
>
> Paul O'Brien, 'Harney Settles Newstalk Libel Case for €450k' *Irish Examiner* (Cork, 5 May 2011)

3.4.10 Interviews

When citing an interview you conducted yourself, give the name, position and institution (as relevant) of the interviewee, and the location and full date of the interview. If the interview was conducted by someone else, the interviewer's name should appear at the beginning of the citation.

> Interview with Irene Kull, Assistant Dean, Faculty of Law, Tartu University (Tartu, Estonia, 4 August 2003)
>
> Timothy Endicott and John Gardner, Interview with Tony Honoré, Emeritus Regius Professor of Civil Law, University of Oxford (Oxford, 17 July 2007)

3.4.11 Personal communications

When citing personal communications, such as emails and letters, give the author and recipient of the communication, and the date. If you are yourself the author or recipient of the communication, say 'from author' or 'to author' as appropriate.

> Letter from Gordon Brown to Lady Ashton (20 November 2009)

Email from Amazon.co.uk to author (16 December 2008)

www.ingramcontent.com/pod-product-compliance
Lightning Source LLC
Chambersburg PA
CBHW072253170526
45158CB00003BA/1067